7 Motivational Marketing Weapons to Win the Battle Against Fear

John Di Lemme

7 Motivational Marketing Weapons to Win the Battle Against Fear

Di Lemme Development Group, Inc.
931 Village Boulevard Suite 905-366
West Palm Beach, Florida 33409-1939
(888) 567-0717
www.ChampionsLiveFree.com

ISBN: 978-1-300-69963-7

About the Author

In September 2001, John Di Lemme founded Di Lemme Development Group, Inc., a company known worldwide for its role in expanding the personal development industry. As President and CEO, John strives for excellence in every area of his business and believes that you must surround yourself with a like-minded team in order to stay on top of your game.

In addition to building a successful company, John has changed lives around the globe as an international motivational speaker that has spoken in over five hundred venues. Over the past eleven years, he has shared the stage with the best of the best including Dr. John Maxwell, Rich Devos, Dennis Waitley, Jim Rohn, and Les Brown only to name a few. John has also been interviewed countless times and featured on many programs including Zig Ziglar's webcast. This is truly an amazing feat for someone that was clinically diagnosed as a stutterer at a very young age and told that he would never speak fluently.

John truly believes that everyone needs personal development to reach their full potential in life, and his determination to reach all forms of media with his motivational messages has catapulted his career. John has produced over four hundred fifty products and is an accomplished author of eleven books including his latest best-selling book, "7 Principles to Live a Champion Life." As a Strategic Business Coach, John's students include doctors, lawyers, entrepreneurs, consultants, CEOs of million dollar companies and various other occupations that are thriving in a so-called poor economy. John's success with his students has made him one of the most highly sought after business coaches in the world.

John's passion is to teach others how to live a champion life despite the label that society has placed on them. Through his books, audio/video materials, sold-out live seminars, numerous television interviews, intensive training boot camps, weekly tele-classes, Strategic Business Coaching, Closing & Marketing University, Millionaire Affirmation Academy, and Lifestyle Freedom Club memberships, John has made success a reality for thousands worldwide.

Introduction

The three major enemies in your life are fear, indecision, and procrastination. They are the enemies of your success that slow down your ability to achieve your Why. When you're fearful and indecisive you procrastinate, "Should I do it? Should I not do it?" You can't move forward, because you are being held back by these enemies.

Fear, indecision and procrastination are activated and/or deactivated by the words that we speak. Many people unconsciously choose to deactivate their miracle through their negative words such as, "This is just who I am. I can't achieve success. That's only for the rich people." Their words instantly activate fear, indecision and procrastination that will ultimately keep them stuck in their same situation. I'm going to teach you seven motivational marketing weapons to win the battle against fear, which is the biggest enemy of our success. Most people are so frozen with fear that it seems impossible for them to even remotely believe that they have the ability to achieve their Why in life. That's why we need weapons to fight fear and annihilate it from our lives.

I love teaching from Navy SEAL books, because of the mindset and discipline it takes to be a Navy SEAL. The mind and body are capable of achieving miracles when there's no way out except to fight. Real enemies exist in the physical realm. That's why we have the United States military and special operation teams like the Navy SEALs.

Right now, there is a rapid increase of weapons being used against our freedom by enemies from around the world. Navy

SEALs are trained to protect that freedom. Even when a Navy SEAL has survived Hell Week, completed years of intense training, and ultimately received his trident, he must still participate in additional trainings. If a Navy SEAL has not been in combat within the last year and he's on active duty, he has to go through another three-week "refresher course." The enemy produces weapons so quickly that just training from a year ago is not going to give a Navy SEAL the extra edge to defeat the enemy.

If the top military forces in the world have to consistently participate in training to fight the enemy, then so do you. Fear is relentless and you must be highly trained and possess weapons to fight it. I'm using the military example, because it's a war out there. We are constantly bombarded by the negative societal views that attempt to label us as how we are seen by others instead of the Champion deep inside that has a right to success.

Once again, you must be trained to fight for your Why. The first step is making sure that you have the needed weapons to protect yourself. So, let's get started!

Motivational Marketing Weapon #1: Commit to Persevere

All of the motivational marketing weapons that I'm going to reveal to you are based on affirmations from my best-selling book, *365 Affirmations to Absolutely Guarantee a Record-Breaking Year*. The first weapon comes from Affirmation #330, which is "I am persevering no matter what anyone else does around me." Perseverance is defined as steady persistence in a course of action especially in spite of difficulties, obstacles, or discouragement. Basically no matter what happens, you don't give up!

In the marketing realm, wouldn't it be nice to deal with a business that persevered in its goal with you? Yes, to actually be there for you as a client and follow through. Unfortunately, that's a rare trait for most businesses these days, but it should be an integral part of your business and who you are as a person.

When a potential customer comes to you for a product or service, you extend your hand to them with confidence knowing that you are there with them until the very end of your course of business even if they choose to do business with someone else. That's right. Even if they don't become your customer, you stand with integrity and make it clear to them that you are there for them.

Right now wherever you are, say this out loud, "I am persevering!" Say it out loud again and truly mean it, "I am persevering!" I don't care what anyone else is doing or who is giving you a strange look. It's your life and your business so start taking action and stand out from the crowd. Let your customers know that you are different and you are ready to enter a long-term, persevering relationship with them.

Motivational Marketing Weapon #2: Be a Conqueror

The second motivational marketing weapon is to be a conqueror. Affirmation #283 states "I am conquering my fears to achieve my dreams." My favorite definition of conqueror is "one that overcomes the enemy." You are overcoming the enemy of fear in your life!

Let me interject here. There's a reason that I continue to give you the definitions of key words in this book. Why? Because if you don't know the meaning behind a particular motivational marketing weapon, then how could you possibly use it? It would be like a Navy SEAL trying to use a weapon that he has never seen before. He may be able to use it after a while, but not as efficiently and effectively with full confidence. Now, let's talk about you becoming a conqueror!

Most people walk around with a defeated mindset. They don't do daily affirmations or any other type of personal development that would enable them to walk with their head high, ready to take on the fear that is holding them back. I used to be one of those people. Stuttering caused me to bury my head in my chest and just hope not be acknowledged by anyone. Fear had stolen my life!

Now, I wake up every day knowing that I have conquered the fear of speaking. I no longer stutter, and I am one of the top international, motivational speakers in the world. What is it that you have to conquer? Make a decision right now that you will overcome and conquer it! The attitude of conquering is critical. If I didn't change my attitude and mindset, I could have never defeated my fear of speaking.

From a marketing perspective, you must conquer the indecision about whether or not you're going to be in business long-term or if your business is going to be successful. If you don't believe in yourself and your business, then your client will have no reason to believe in you. There's absolutely no way that you can build a business with such a defeatist mindset.

I recently read an article in *The Wall Street Journal*, which basically stated that the problem in the United States is not the economy. It's a trust issue that has created a crisis for our businesses. Trust in business comes from doing what you say that you are going to do for your customers on a consistent basis. Yes, it's that easy. Just keep your promise and do the right thing!

I'm sure that the United States isn't the only country with a trust issue among businesses and their customers. So, if you live outside of America, don't think you are excluded. This is a worldwide issue that is killing our ability to build highly successful businesses and develop healthy, long-term relationships with our clients.

How do we overcome this trust issue? You must separate yourself and your business from the crowd by conquering the fear that is preventing you from exuding confidence to your potential clients and gaining their trust. Over-deliver for your clients and do the right thing. Be on time. Dress for success. Actively listen to what they want. Thank them for their business. Follow up. These are just the basics that will create a rock-solid foundation for your business and give your clients a reason to trust you.

Being a conqueror will radically change your life and business. You are no longer standing in the shadows, because you have faced your fears. People will take notice and will be eager to find out why your business is so different from the rest.

Motivational Marketing Weapon #3: Have a Strategic Plan

Affirmation #280 is "I am building a lifelong strategic plan of action to accomplish my mission." Do you have a strategic plan in place every day to receive and achieve supernatural miraculous eyeball-popping, people-stopping, jaw-dropping, abundant overflow in your life? If you don't have a plan, then how are you going to achieve your desired result?

We live in a society where people want a life of convenience. We've all been in need of something before and make the decision to grab it at the local convenience store even if we have to pay more. It's convenient and gives us instant gratification. Similarly, if we live a life of convenience, then we will definitely pay more for success and the instant gratification will only feel good for a little while.

For example, let's say that you want to lose weight. Instead of a healthy diet and exercise, you grab the latest, greatest diet pill on the market. You lose twenty pounds in two weeks and you love how you look.

However within a few weeks, the side effects of the pill start to kick in and you stop taking it. You gain all of the weight back plus more and you are continually sick at your stomach. The pill was convenient, but you paid more for that convenience by gaining weight and jeopardizing your health plus the instant gratification didn't satisfy you long-term.

Just think if you would have chosen to implement a healthy strategic plan of action to lose the weight. You would have lost weight gradually and developed healthy habits that last a life-time. That's a very clear cut example of having a strategic plan of action versus a quick fix solution.

How does this apply to your business? It's the exact same. You must have a strategic plan of action for building a successful business. Your intentional daily preparation will help you to maintain consistent focus going forward and keep you from flip flopping from one thing to another looking for a quick fix.

Your plan will change over time as your business grows, but the first step is to implement a strategic plan of action, which includes the basic fundamentals that we discussed in the previous chapter – be on time, dress for success, etc. Remember, there are no shortcuts or quick fixes for success. Do it the right way now so you don't pay more later!

Motivational Marketing Weapon #4: Develop a Learning Habit

The next motivational marketing weapon comes from Affirmation #51, "I am increasing my learning daily to achieve my Why now." What is your learning habit? Are you constantly learning something new every day that moves you close towards the achievement of your Why?

One of my goals is to build the first billion dollar self-development company. That's the reason I study multi-billion dollar companies and share the stories of companies like HSN, Disney, AOL, Dell, Starbucks, and Amazon with the members of the Closing and Marketing University. It's incredibly important for me and my students to know how these businesses were built from the ground up.

Billion dollar industry leaders like Howard Schultz and Jeff Bezos aren't named Fortune Magazine's top CEOs, because they run mom-and-pop businesses. They paid the price and developed billion dollar strategies that have changed the world. That gets my attention and makes me eager to learn from their success and failures.

Learning is a motivational marketing weapon because most of the people around you are not learning. They stay stuck in the rut of doing what everyone else is doing despite the fact that everyone around them is failing. When you increase your learning, you go out into the world refreshed and eager to take on new challenges because you know that someone else has gone before you and done what you want to do. It removes the impossible, which is half the battle of building a business.

Start your learning habit by reading, listening to, or watching something that inspires you for only fifteen minutes a day. Why only fifteen minutes? Because it's easy to develop a habit a little bit at a time. If you rush into it like most people, then you won't get past day one. Commit to the fifteen minutes per day and then build upon that as you go. Before you know it, you will be chomping at the bit to learn more about the things that will take you to the next level in your life and business.

Motivational Marketing Weapon #5: Never Again

Two of the most powerful words in success language are "never again." Affirmation #65 is "Never again will I retreat when the enemy of fear attacks my dream." Never means *not ever and at no time.* When the enemy of fear knows you will not back down and you will never retreat again, you are already one step ahead.

How many times have you retreated? How many times have you bowed down the enemy of fear? Close your eyes and imagine a time that something was too hard and you ran away instead of facing it. Fear got its grips in you and you fled. Do it now. Close your eyes and imagine a time that happened to you.

Now open your eyes and say this out loud, "Never again will I retreat when the enemy of fear attacks my dream!" Say it again. Doesn't that feel good? Never again!

Remember, it doesn't make a difference what anybody else is doing or what type of business you own. You will NEVER AGAIN back down from fear. You will NEVER AGAIN be a follower in failure. When you vow to NEVER AGAIN be the pawn of the enemy of fear, you will unleash a wave of power in your life that nothing can stop.

When you choose not retreat, miracles will show up at your door. Knock. Knock. Who's there? Your supernatural miracle is standing at your door, because you didn't flee from the enemy. Do you believe it? Do you truly believe and receive the absolute fact that when you stand up for yourself and your Why that great things will start to happen?

I know it's uncomfortable, because you've always ran away before so you weren't able to see the miracles that were waiting for you. You are different now and you have made a declaration that NEVER AGAIN will you retreat. So, start looking for your supernatural miracles!

Motivational Marketing Weapon #6: Organized, Forward-Moving, Construction Zone

This is a very controversial weapon and comes from Affirmation #69, "I am living in an organized forward-moving, profitable, life-changing construction zone." Weapon #6 is an "organized, forward-moving, construction zone." If you're not personally organized, then you'll never be able to bring organization to your business. All of my top students that are experiencing supernatural miracles in their life have an organized, forward-moving construction zone. I said construction zone not a destruction zone.

Let's take Dorcie Farkash for instance. Dorcie's construction zone at TW Design is a clean, inviting space that empowers her to build her business. Her affirmations are posted on the wall in front of her and she is surrounded by photos of her family. She refers to it as her construction zone not her office, because the word "office" has a negative connotation. Dorcie is building her billion dollar, life-changing business in her organized, forward-moving construction zone.

What if I knocked on your door right now and asked to take a look at your construction zone? What would I see? Is it organized and forward-moving or is it a complete mess that makes your feel trapped? If you're living in clutter and disorganization, you will never succeed. No questions asked. You will absolutely never succeed.

One of the biggest barriers that I often see to an organized, forward-moving construction zone is the "just in case" mindset. You have all kinds of garbage cluttering your space "just in case" you ever need it. There's no way that you can be organized if you can't let go of useless stuff that you no longer need. Go into your construction zone right now. Are you there? If not, go in there now. If you can't, then close your eyes and imagine your construction zone. What do you see? Do you see a bunch of stuff that you haven't used in six months or longer? If so, get rid of it!

Give it all away or if it has absolutely no value, then throw it away. If you are saving stuff for that "just in case" moment in life that never comes, then just quit. That's right. I said it. Just quit, because I don't want you to be under the false assumption that you are going to achieve success while you are sitting in a dump that you call your office. Is that harsh? Yes, but it's true. Clutter controls you and your destiny!

If you even dare to mumble under your breath, "Well, I wonder what his construction zone looks like?" Let me just tell you straight up that you couldn't handle my construction zone. It's an organized, forward-moving, miracle-creating machine! Right in front of me I have my original dream board from 1990 which says, "John Di Lemme has built a billion dollar company on guts and service." Yes, I've been looking at that miraculous declaration since 1990, and I have no doubt in my mind that it's going to happen. What have you been looking at for the last twenty years? If you say nothing, then guess what you are going to achieve...nothing! But the good news is that you can change that by creating your own dream board in your new organized, forward-moving construction zone.

I want to give you a bonus affirmation that ties into this motivational marketing weapon. Affirmation #108 declares "I am eliminating all distractions now in my life to ultimately live my why." When you have an organized, forward-moving construction zone, there are no distractions that will stop you from achieving your supernatural miracle or coming up with that supernatural idea that will forever change your business.

Before you go any further in this book, I want you to get busy on your organized, forward-moving construction zone. Don't allow it to overwhelm you. Take fifteen minutes per day to get rid of unneeded stuff and then start building your dream board of daily affirmations, photos and anything else that empowers you to achieve your Why. I want to see it when you are done so send a photo to John@LifestyleFreedomClub.com.

Motivational Marketing Weapon #7: Change Your Habits

Last but not least, the final weapon comes from Affirmation #121, "My habits predict supernatural miracles." Habit is defined as "a usual or established behavior." Basically, it's something that you do all the time without much thought. It's second nature.

What are your habits? What's that one thing that is second nature or just comes naturally? For example, if you were to throw a basketball to Michael Jordan, he would catch it. Even if he was in the middle of a conversation, he would likely catch the ball without thinking about it. It comes natural to him, because he's been doing it his entire life. For years, he practiced and trained to be one of the very best basketball players in history. My favorite Michael Jordan quote is

"If you quit once, it becomes a habit. Never quit!" He fully understands that one decision will develop a habit that could change the course of your future. Michael Jordan's success lies in his daily habits and refusal to quit.

Now, let me ask you again. What are your habits? Take a minute to think about what you do every day that has become a developed habit – good or bad. For me, it's exercise and self-development. No matter where I am in the world I will exercise and do my self-development, which I like to call my Morning Miracle Preparation. I drink a gallon of water every day without hesitation. These are my habits that empower me to face my day with strength and live in an atmosphere of supernatural expectation that miracles will happen in my life.

Unfortunately, the word “habit” has a negative undertone. When most people think of a habit, they reflect on the self-destructive things that they do in life such as smoking, drinking, laziness, etc. When you shift your focus from bad habits to good ones, your life will change and most of those bad habits will fade away.

For instance, if you make a decision to create a new daily habit of eating healthy and exercising every day, then it will be harder for you to continue smoking and drinking. The two habits just simply don’t go together and it’s hard for them to coexist. In the end, one habit will win over the other, and it’s your decision as to which one it will be.

Similarly in business, fear and faith cannot go hand in hand. The enemy of fear cannot live in the faith zone, where you are saying your daily affirmations, immersing yourself in daily personal development, building your business on a solid foundation of integrity, and focusing on long-term relationships with your clients. Those are just a few habits that annihilate the enemy of fear.

Once you've established your faith zone and those daily habits come second nature to you, I guarantee your customers will take notice and your business will explode. There's no stopping the supernatural miracles that will occur in your life once you make the decision to change your habits.

Conclusion

I encourage you to write out all of the 7 Motivational Marketing Weapons and the individual affirmations so that you can put them in your organized, forward-moving construction zone. Post them right in front of you so the weapons are handy when you face a battle. Declare the affirmations over your life every single day as part of your new Morning Miracle Preparation. I believe in you and know that you will conquer the enemy of fear!

www.ingramcontent.com/pod-product-compliance
Ingram Content Group UK Ltd.
Pitfield, Milton Keynes, MK11 3LW, UK
UKHW020215250726
13967UKWH00001B/3

9 781300 699637